BRITISH RAILW

PAST and PRESENT

No 12

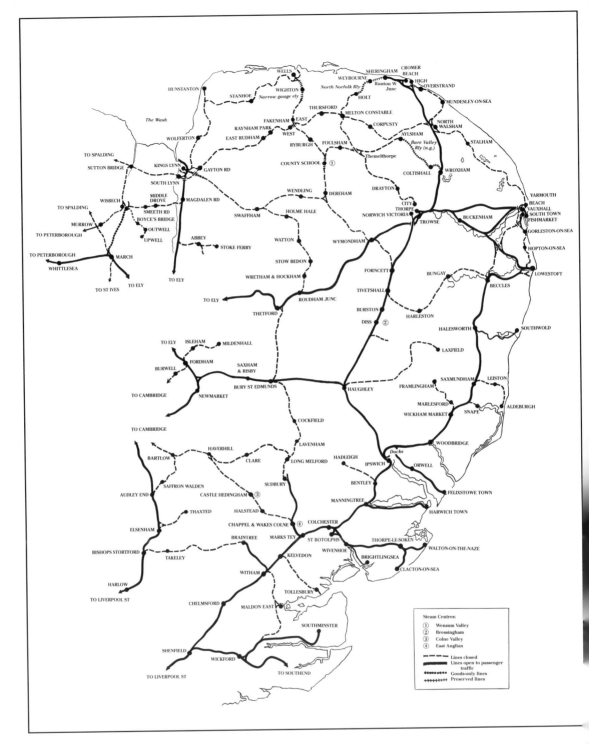

BRITISH RAILWAYS PAST & PRESENT No 12: EAST ANGLIA — This book presents a detailed examination of the changing face of the railways in the region depicted in this map, which shows locations featured in the photographs or mentioned in the text. The pictures have been chosen to provide a balanced view, including railways which are still in use or being developed, together with scenes where the lines have been closed and either abandoned or redeveloped since the 'past' pictures were taken.

BRITISH RAILWAYS

PAST and PRESENT

No 12

East Anglia

Norfolk, Suffolk and North Essex

Des Saunders & Richard Adderson

Past & Present Publishing Ltd

First published in 1992
Reprinted 1994
Reprinted 2001

British Library Cataloguing in Publication Data

A catalogue record for this book is available from the British Library

ISBN 1 85895 056 2

Past and Present Publishing Ltd
The Trundle
Ringstead Road
Great Addington
Kettering
Northants
NN14 4BW

Tel/Fax: 01536 330588
email: sales@nostalgiacollection.com
Website: www.nostalgiacollection.com

Printed and bound in Great Britain

To Aunt Win,
without whom this book
would not have been possible.

MANNINGTREE: East Anglian local passenger, 'fifties style. 'B12/3' 4-6-0 No 61523 rumbles over the River Stour at Manningtree with an up stopping train; the clerestory-roofed coach behind the tender is particularly noteworthy *H. N. James*

CONTENTS

Main-line freight, 'nineties style. Railfreight-liveried 90038, one of a class becoming increasingly common on freightliner traffic on the GE main line, heads an up working over the Stour on a dull 21 June 1991. The basic structure of the bridge is little altered, but today carries a load undreamed of by its builders. *RJA*

STOW BEDON: It was perhaps surprising that the very rural line from Thetford to Swaffham lasted as long as it did, but it could not survive the Beeching Report, closing in June 1964, although a limited goods service from Swaffham to Watton lingered on until April 1965. On 13 June 1964, the last day of passenger services, the 2.25 from Swaffham runs over the level crossing to pick up its single passenger at Stow Bedon.

Nothing much is left here today; one has to depend on an Ordnance Survey map, preferably an old one. The old station yard is now the entrance to the circular Pingles walk of some 8 miles, utilising part of the Peddars Way and returning via the old trackbed. The massive concrete post of the level crossing gate is the only clue that a railway once ran here; the rest of the site is a wilderness, while across the road is a dwelling house, formerly a pub. Nature-lovers may be interested to know that the Great Eastern Pingle Trail project was opened by Norfolk County Council in conjunction with the Countryside Commission, the Norfolk Naturalists Trust and the Manpower Services Commission, and the part along the old line is particularly noted for its diversity of butterflies. *RJA/DGS*

INTRODUCTION

Geographically and historically there have been many widely varied definitions of East Anglia — some 'regional' media would include Northampton and Corby within its boundaries. From a railway point of view, the area can reasonably be described as the territory served by the former Great Eastern Railway, with the obvious exception of the London suburban lines, thus taking in all of Norfolk and Suffolk, most of Essex and parts of Cambridgeshire.

Quite where suburbia ends and East Anglia begins is open to debate, and probably varies as London's influence spreads ever wider to take in what were once undoubtedly provincial areas. We have to start somewhere, so we have drawn an imaginary east-west line through Southminster, Chelmsford and Harlow; south of this line is 'London', northwards lies the 'East Anglia' which is covered in this book.

First we will take what is now the 'West Anglia' main line of Network SouthEast to Kings Lynn, and also look at some lines in the west of the region which did not survive to the days of red lamp-posts. Having reached the North Norfolk coast at Hunstanton, we return again to 'Outer Suburbia', to the lines through Colchester to Clacton, Harwich and Ipswich. Getting away from commuterland, we then look at the fascinating network of rural lines on the Essex/Suffolk/Cambridgeshire borders, before continuing northwards along the East Suffolk line and the main line to Norwich.

Our tour of Norfolk will reveal that this county, being essentially a rural area, has suffered more than most in the way of railway closures, but at the time of writing the surviving lines would appear to have a secure future.

With all due respect to the Southwold, Mid Suffolk and Colne Valley & Halstead railways, it was only in Norfolk that the GER had any real competition. This was in the form of the Midland & Great Northern Joint Railway, which ran from Yarmouth across the county to Kings Lynn and ultimately on to Peterborough and the Midlands. Formed in 1893 by the amalgamation of a number of locally promoted lines, the 'Joint', as it became known, handled heavy traffic over largely single track in its heyday. With the exception of a few freight spurs, though, the 'Joint's' 182 route miles were closed completely on 28 February 1959 — perhaps the first major railway closure in the country, and long before the infamous Doctor Beeching appeared on the scene.

In the 'fifties and 'sixties, when the majority of the 'past' photographs in this book were taken, there was of course considerable variety in the railway scene, and it was this variety which was the attraction to many enthusiasts of that era. With trains likely to be formed of a rich selection of rolling-stock anything up to 40 years old, and to be hauled by any one of a number of locomotive classes, there was a sense of anticipation to see what would actually turn up. On the other hand, there was an air of permanence about the stations, where in many cases ancient lamps and signs dating back to pre-Grouping days lasted well into the 1950s.

By and large it is the opposite which applies today, as there is an unprecedented degree of uniformity and predictability in the trains themselves. To us, while visiting locations for this book, the uncertainty and anticipation was not about the type of train we would see, but more about how things had changed. Would it be possible to find a similar viewpoint to yesteryear? Would any of yesteryear's features still be there, or would the 'bus shelter'-type buildings and overhead catenary have removed all traces? In many cases, of course, we knew we would not see any trains, and here the question was even more basic — would there be anything to see there at all, or would a road improvement scheme or industrial estate have obliterated the site entirely? But when we were able to find features to link the photographs, whether obvious or not, the sense of satisfaction for both of us was no less than it would have been if, in the old days, a 'J15' and two ancient coaches had appeared instead of the expected diesel railcar.

In a project of this sort there are two main enemies, nature and man. We think that East Anglia can lay claim to as many, if not more, closed railway lines than any other part of the country, and consequently this book perhaps more than others in the series has a greater portion of 'shock' comparisons, which is where nature and man come into the picture. There are some locations where it is impossible to reach the same spot short of having a machete or bulldozer.

The tell-tale remains of railways are everywhere in East Anglia, to your left and right — that line of post-and-wire fencing for no apparent reason enclosing a line of scrub-land crossing the road where a small gatekeeper's cottage remains, once the basic accommodation for a man and wife on duty sometimes round the clock.

We found that the production of an old photograph was a key that opened many doors; the vast majority of owner-occupiers were only too happy to show us around, point out remaining memorabilia, and show, in their opinion, the exact spot where the previous photograph was taken. Present-day railwaymen for the most part were very interested, the older men particularly wallowing in nostalgia.

We would like to place on record our sincere thanks to all who contributed to this book by generously lending us their valuable photographic records, and for their interest and willingness to assist in any way; to my wife who accompanied me to the far corners of East Anglia on every trip, and undertook the not inconsiderable task of typing the manuscript; and also the current owners of private railway stations, who afforded us every facility to photograph their houses from all angles.

Des Saunders
Fakenham

Richard Adderson
Norwich

A different variation on the 'past and present' theme: tickets from the M&GN, Great Eastern and British Railways eras compared with the tickets issued on the same lines in the 1990s. *RJA*

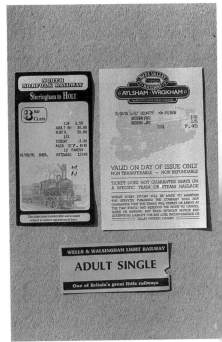

West Anglia

HARLOW: The couple canoodling underneath the gas lamp are about to be disturbed by the passage of 'Britannia' 4-6-2 No 70037 *Hereward the Wake* as it hammers through the station with an up express on 2 June 1956. At this time the route was used not only by the trains between Hunstanton, Kings Lynn and London, but by certain of the Norwich trains too.

Despite electrification, there are only detail differences to the station building at Harlow in June 1991. The station has now been renamed Harlow Mill as it is some distance from the New Town development, and the former Burnt Mill station, closer to the New Town, has become Harlow Town. A 1960s design signal box has replaced the traditional box, and has taken over the duties of several manual boxes in the area, whilst the Cambridge main line is now multiple unit territory, and the days of prestige expresses have gone. A Class '317' EMU, typical of the 1991 scene, glides under the road bridge, the latter having been rebuilt to give clearance for the catenary. *H.C. Casserley/RJA*

BISHOPS STORTFORD: A rake of Gresley coaches headed by 'B12/3' 4-6-0 No 61547 threads the complex trackwork at Bishops Stortford on 8 September 1956. The train is the up 'Holiday Camps Express' from Caister-on-Sea, which has made a long and circuitous journey north via the M&GN to North Walsham, south again to Norwich, west to Ely, and now the returning holidaymakers have another 30 miles to go before arriving at Liverpool Street.

In May 1991 a Class '317' EMU heads for Liverpool Street over much simplified trackwork compared with the earlier picture. The semaphore signals are gone, of course, and the ever-present catenary is much in evidence; however, the South signal box is still a feature of the railway scene. I could not manage quite the same spot because of BR's 'shrubbery', having to move a few yards to the left. *R.C. Riley/DGS*

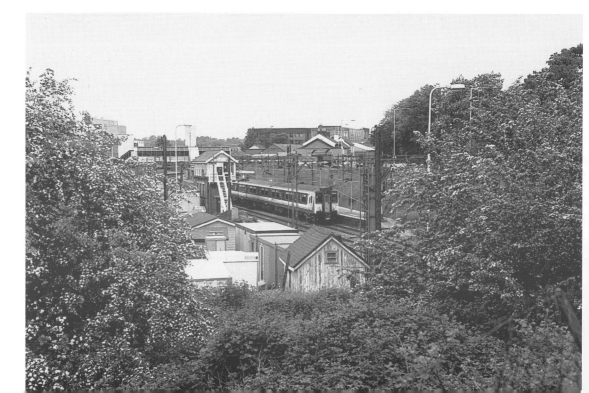

ELSENHAM: 'B1' 4-6-0 No 61286 approaches the down platform at Elsenham with a stopping train on 30 June 1951. The ancient lamps, cast-iron signs and the neat gardens on the up platform are all typical of the period.

On 28 May 1991, Class '317' EMU No 317366 speeds through the station with a Liverpool Street to Cambridge train. Elsenham today is a busy wayside station with very little in the way of stopping trains outside rush hours, but I noticed some commuter traffic and the level crossing gates are busy. An enthusiastic railway employee (ex-fireman) told me that the telegraph pole was only cut down a couple of years ago, and pointed out the stump left in the ground which is still just visible in the photograph behind the white gate under the 'Way out' sign. *H.C. Casserley/DGS*

AUDLEY END: A down Cambridge line stopping train drifts into Audley End station behind 'L1' 2-6-4T No 67723 on 30 June 1951. Beyond the goods yard is the junction with the Saffron Walden line (see page 59), and a signal on this line can be seen to the left of the tank wagons. Branch trains terminated at a separate platform behind the somewhat rickety sheds.

There is a feel of commuterland about this station today, a full car park having replaced the goods yard and branch line platform. Class '317' EMU No 317324 hurries a train through Audley End on its way to Cambridge; most of these units are based at Hornsey EMUD. *H.C. Casserley/DGS*

BURWELL: On 11 June 1962, just five days before closure, Railbus E79964 pauses at Burwell station, between Cambridge and Fordham, on its way to Mildenhall. Although the railbuses cut operating costs on the branch, the passing loop, signals and station staff were, in hindsight, something of an extravagance as traffic declined.

An enquiry at a local club led to the site of the station, now as so often an industrial complex. Investigation of the car park revealed the cottage seen in the earlier picture now looking old and neglected. Many of these present-day photographs will be almost impossible to take in a few years' time. *RJA/DGS*

ISLEHAM, on the Fordham–Mildenhall branch, and the waiting room and canopies have a marked similarity to those just encountered up the line at Burwell. Again the railwaymen pass the time of day as they wait for the photographer to rejoin the same railbus for the last leg of the journey to Mildenhall.

The station house here is in private occupation with an adjacent tyre centre, but the garden is well kept and at the end of the lawn stands the road bridge, looking remarkably good for its age. *RJA/DGS*

MILDENHALL: In the late 1950s the Mildenhall branch achieved a degree of fame in enthusiast circles as the last haunt of the ex-GER 'Intermediate' 2-4-0s, by then BR Class 'E4'. One of these Cambridge-based locos, No 62785, leaves the terminus at the head of the 5.40 pm to Newmarket on 3 May 1958, with a Great Eastern coach behind the tender. Fortunately this loco was preserved and now forms part of the National Collection.

A very spacious and grand building is the station house here, well looked after and in private ownership. As the terminus of a country branch line which never made much money, the scale of the building is rather surprising. Somewhere under the lawn is the site of the turntable and signal box. *R.C. Riley/DGS*

ABBEY: In October 1965 Abbey station, on the Stoke Ferry branch, was still neat and tidy although it had lost its original canopy, following the withdrawal of the passenger service in 1930. It remained in use as the junction for the Wissington Light Railway, serving a sugar beet factory, until the early 1980s, although the line on to Stoke Ferry had closed completely in April 1965. One of the Wissington Railway steam locos can be seen at the platform end; during the sugar beet season long freight trains were commonplace.

This sparsely populated area was never going to make a profit for a railway and today only a short length of platform remains and a small corrugated hut on the platform. Just out of sight, the crossing keeper's cottage and station master's house appear to be in good order and in private occupation; a notice proclaims 'Trials Moto X Circuit, Station Farm', and a telephone number. *RJA/DGS*

STOKE FERRY: As already noted, passenger services on the branch from Denver were early victims of the LNER's economy drive, being withdrawn in 1930. Occasional goods trains continued to run until 1965, but this was almost certainly the final visit of a passenger train to the terminus. Class '4MT' 2-6-0 No 43149, having made a welcome return visit to its former M&GN haunts at East Rudham earlier in the day, pulls in with a special on 26 May 1962.

In 1991 the station house is occupied and in a good state of repair, whilst a timber firm occupies the track area. Had passenger receipts been greater the line would have been extended to the small village of Gooderstone, but in the event the proposed extension would have done nothing to lengthen the life of the branch. *Both RJA*

MAGDALEN ROAD (now called WATLINGTON): Leaving some of its wagons on the down main line, a 'J19' 0-6-shunts the pick-up goods in the yard. The main line to Ely disappears straight ahead into the Fenland mists, whil the branch to Wisbech and March curves away behind the platelayers hut.

The Cambridge-bound DMU discharged a handful of passengers, but then it was market day down the line i Kings Lynn. The wires are up as far as Kings Lynn, but I am informed that the switch-on will not be until the sprin of 1992. The station closed in 1968 but reopened seven years later; it is now called Watlington, but the signal bo stubbornly remains Magdalen Road, due, I was told, to some sort of hitch in the byelaws. The trackbed of th branch to Wisbech veers to the right where the van is parked, and a short length of the goods platform can clearl be seen; on the left a small estate of houses has sprung up. *Norfolk Railway Society Archive/DGS*

MIDDLE DROVE: The line from Magdalen Road across the flat fenland to Wisbech opened as early as 1848. Middle Drove was the first station on the branch, and its rather basic facilities are seen here as a 'J17' 0-6-0 rumbles through with an ancient van in tow.

Another lonely spot, seen on a dreary autumn afternoon, but station house and shelter on the down side are still intact, the platform sloping away into a ploughed field. 'It will cost you 50p,' said the young lady coming out of the station house. 'Dad would like a chat about the station. I'll get him.' But unfortunately Dad did not emerge.
D. Thompson/DGS

SMEETH ROAD: Taken at around the time of nationalisation, this study of Smeeth Road typifies the rural branch-line station, and with only detail differences could have been taken at any time during the previous 30 years.

When I visited the former station in the autumn of 1990, the owner of the signal box and waiting room (known as 'Annie's room' in this part of the world) was delighted when I showed him the photograph of the station taken some 30 years before, and immediately offered to buy it from me. We settled for swapping addresses. He then showed us a Midland six-wheel coach splendidly converted to a cosy office; he has plans to convert the signal box to a hairdressing salon — surely a first — while the 18-lever frame, still in situ, is going to the Nene Valley Railway. Apparently it was a rule that all signal boxes in this area had a Bible kept in them. *D. Thompson/DGS*

WISBECH EAST: By the time this picture was taken in 1967, the writing was very much on the wall for the March to Magdalen Road line, and Wisbech East station had a run-down and neglected air about it. An LNER Thompson-designed coach is the first vehicle of this March-bound train as it leaves the weed-strewn platform behind Brush Type 2 No D5633. The Upwell tram used the outer face of the island platform and the different profile of the platform is still noticeable.

This is a site which is not too easy to locate now. A gentleman cutting his hedge obligingly showed my wife and I a book with an aerial photograph, on which we were able to pick out the existing houses in relation to the station. The whole site is covered by a complex called the Octavia Hill Centre for the handicapped. I remarked that the whole rebuilt area already had a mature look but, as our companion reminded us, the demolition of the station took place 20 years ago. . . *A.C. Ingram/DGS*

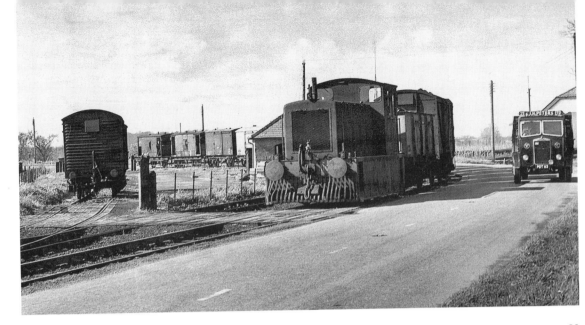

BOYCES BRIDGE: The Wisbech & Upwell Tramway served its agricultural community well enough for some 80 years after the first train ran in 1882. Although passenger services were withdrawn in 1928, the goods service soldiered on until 1966. The original steam tram engines (see opposite) were replaced very early in the diesel era by similarly enclosed Drewry 0-6-0 diesel shunters, one of which, No 11102, pauses at Boyces Bridge depot on 27 March 1957. Although the train is well loaded, the passing lorry is a sign of the ever-increasing movement of freight by road transport.

Becoming more and more of an anachronism with each passing year, the Wisbech & Upwell eventually closed in May 1966, and the tracks were removed a few years later. Few traces of the line remain in 1991, but the unmistakeably 'railway' gate which used to control the siding entrance still stands in the waste ground which was once Boyces Bridge depot. *W.J. Naunton/RJA*

OUTWELL: One of the distinctive steam tram locos, the inspiration for Rev Awdry's 'Toby', provides entertainment for the village children at Outwell in the very early days.

This was another difficult spot to find, especially on a dreary wet spring afternoon. Yesteryear's picture has a claim to be the oldest in this book, but enquiries at a local Club saw us correctly to the location. The buildings on the right are much the same, the two houses in the distance remain and, although the trains may have stopped, the canal beyond still flows. Sadly, though, I am sure that none of the children are still with us. *A.C. Ingram/DGS*

MARCH was the 'frontier post' for East Anglia, with the majority of the freight from the North and Midlands passing through, or being remarshalled in the busy and extensive yards at Whitemoor. The town's railway importance was also reflected by a thriving locomotive depot. The 'new shed' at the locomotive depot was built in 1932, being intended as a running shed for the quick turn-round of engines at this important railway centre. To the right of the shed is the boiler house and its chimney, whilst to the left is the ponderously titled 'Illuminated Loco Inspection Pit'. Commonly known as the 'light tunnel', this was provided to simplify the task of loco inspection during the blackout conditions of the Second World War. At the time that this picture was taken, 29 July 1975, the shed yard was being used for wagon repair work.

The general air of desolation in the March area has been heightened in recent years by the use of the yards for dumping withdrawn locomotives. By 4 October 1987 the shed building and most of the boiler house had been demolished, but the 'light tunnel', with its distinctive striped door, was still standing. Locomotives had, however, returned to the shed area, but the rows of Class '45' and Class '20' diesels are rusting on the grass-grown tracks. Prominent in the foreground are Nos 45029, 45040 and 45066. *Both D.C. Pearce*

WHITTLESEA: With the sidings, goods dock, lamp hut, loading gauge and traditional signal box, there was something of the atmosphere of bygone years at Whittlesea, on the March–Peterborough line, as late as May 1982. Regrettably, though, the gricers 'flailing' from the front coach of the train are very much a product of the contemporary scene! Two of the dwindling fleet of Class '40' diesels, Nos 40012 and 40081, double-head the 'Anglian Whistler' railtour towards Peterborough.

In 1991 the signal box surveys a much bleaker scene, as a Class '156' 'Sprinter' passes. The goods dock siding looks neglected and ready for removal, and the other features have been demolished. Even the signal on the left has lost its white sighting panel. *D.C. Pearce/DGS*

KINGS LYNN (1): On 23 June 1958 'N7' 0-6-2T No 69620 busies itself shunting parcels stock in the centre roads at Kings Lynn station. At this time the station was a busy place, handling services on the lines to Hunstanton, Norwich, March, Ely and South Lynn.

Thirty-three years later the only passenger service to survive is that to Cambridge, connecting with the electric service on to London, although through services to London should resume with electrification in 1992. The overhead wires and masts are in place, and the trackwork has been rationalised, but the basic structure of the station from this viewpoint has changed but little over the years. *R.C. Riley/DGS*

KINGS LYNN (2): Days of transition at Kings Lynn — 'B12/3' 4-6-0 No 61514 runs into the station with a long parcels train on 6 August 1959 whilst two other steam locos darken the sky outside the loco shed to the left. The presence of Brush Type 2 diesel No D5534 standing alongside the signal box is an indication of things to come.

Thirty-two years later transition is again in the air, and the diesels are on their way out as Kings Lynn station waits for the electric era to begin. With the overhead wiring in place, a three-car Class '101' DMU heads for Cambridge over much reduced trackwork. The box and the fine signal gantries have been gone for many years, whilst the loco shed area is now the station car park. Presumably the platform will be widened to coincide with the re-aligned track! Ironically, at the time that this picture was taken, a poster on the station was advertising the forthcoming visit of three steam locos to the line. The wheel has come full circle! *A.E. Bennett/RJA*

WOLFERTON: On a bright winter morning in 1950 the Royal Train stands at Wolferton station on the Royal Estate awaiting King George VI and Queen Elizabeth, at the end of their traditional Christmas holiday at Sandringham. The loco is one of the 'Clauds' kept especially clean by Kings Lynn depot for Royal Train duties — a Cambridge 'Sandringham' Class 4-6-0 was maintained in a similar condition for the same purpose. Even after the run-down and closure of the Hunstanton line, royalty continued to travel as far as Kings Lynn by rail, often in a special coach attached to a normal service train, before finishing their journey to Sandringham by road. Whether royal patronage will continue when the Kings Lynn line is operated by outer suburban electric multiple units is open to question.

Following closure, the buildings on the up platform were converted to residential use, whilst the down platform buildings now house a railway museum, with particular emphasis on Royal Train travel. As a result the ornate buildings remain in a good state of repair, and continue to blend well with their surroundings. *Eastern Daily Press/RJA*

HUNSTANTON: The railway from Kings Lynn reached Hunstanton in 1862, and the town grew rapidly from then on. Its station, right next to the sea, handled heavy traffic for a century, with regular through trains from London and summer excursions from the Midlands terminating at the two island platforms. Two 'D16/3' 4-4-0s, Nos 62524 (tender first) and 62597, wait at Hunstanton on 6 August 1959; this was something of a scoop for the photographer, as only 13 of this well-loved and once-numerous class still survived at that time. The air of prosperity, however, is misleading; less than a decade later the line had closed entirely, the last train running over the singled track into a forlorn terminus in May 1969.

Now the station area is a car park, with the flat-roofed building on the right, and the adjoining double chimney pots, providing a link between the two views. *A.E. Bennett/DGS*

Outer Suburbia

WICKFORD: Ex-GER 'B12/3' Class No 61557 on a Liverpool Street to Southend train arrives at Wickford Junction in February 1955.

Some 35 years later Class '321/3' No 321309 pulls into the station with today's equivalent, an evening Liverpool Street to Southend Victoria train. Amongst all the changes, the telegraph pole in the centre of the picture survives as does the fencing. Commuter country again here — in fact, at the southernmost point of our area we have the signs of a healthy railway these days; the former yards are now a car park. I wonder if the elderly gentleman caught his train eventually. *T.J. Edgington/DGS*

SOUTHMINSTER: Class 'N7/5' No 69630 waits at the Southminster terminus with a Liverpool Street train. These 0-6-2 tank engines bore the brunt of the suburban and semi-fast trains to the east and north-east of London.

Unfortunately, when I visited the station in May 1991 there was no train, the next one was not due for 45 minutes and I had a heavy schedule to complete. However, I was impressed by the overall appearance, neat and tidy, with the digital clock whirring away above my head — these seem to be a common feature on modern stations. *T.J. Edgington/DGS*

CHELMSFORD: A two-car Cravens diesel multiple unit runs into Chelmsford station from the north, passing a rake of electric multiple unit stock awaiting its next turn of duty. At this time, 28 September 1958, Chelmsford was the northern extremity of electric working from Liverpool Street. Neither of the pictured trains was more than a year or two old when the photograph was taken, and the scene very much conveys the 'modern image' which British Railways was trying to create at the time.

Thirty-three years on, a later generation of electric multiple unit stock is represented by a Class '312' set running in on an up train. As part of the modernisation of the station, the up platform has been extended, and the siding is no longer needed as the electric services now reach more northerly points. Surprisingly, perhaps, the water tower and distant square chimney still overlook the changed scene. *A.E. Bennett/RJA*

WITHAM: 'Britannia' 'Pacific' No 70036 *Boadicea* runs into Witham with an up express on 21 November 1959. Judging from the air of anticipation on the platform, the train is probably going to call here, allowing an interchange with the branch-line services to Braintree (see page 34) and to Maldon (see page 36).

In 1991 the scene is far more functional — even the traditional maltings have been enlarged out of all recognition. The large water tank and lofty signal box on the left have been swept away to make room for an extension of the down platform; the area is now controlled by a large signal box of 1960s design behind the up platform. Working push-pull, a Class '86' electric hurtles through the station at the rear of a down Norwich express. *A.E. Bennett/DGS*

BRAINTREE: The most southerly of the east-west routes connecting the Ipswich and Cambridge main lines was tha from Witham to Bishops Stortford, opening in 1869. Passenger services west of Braintree were withdrawn in th early 1950s; later in that decade a Derby lightweight DMU is seen at Braintree — the pre-war Ford 8 was old eve then. The truncated branch line was listed for closure in the Beeching Report, by which time a four-wheel railbu was often sufficient to cope with the passengers.

However, increasing commuter traffic revived the line's fortunes, to the extent that it was electrified in 1977, an trains now run through to London. The line is now single tracked, the down station buildings having gone. Th Booking Clerk here was most interested in the collection of photographs that I had with me. *Lens of Sutton/DGS*

TAKELEY: Participants in a Railway Club brake-van special inspect Takeley station on 12 September 1959, as 'J19' No 64646 waits at the platform with their train. Despite the tidy appearance of the station, passenger trains had been withdrawn between Braintree and Bishops Stortford seven years earlier.

Nestling almost under a road bridge, the station house still seems to be occupied. The line ran parallel to the busy A120 and one wonders, with the present reappraisal of transport, whether this line should not have been retained! *R.C. Riley/DGS*

MALDON EAST: Passenger trains on the branch line from Witham to the imposing terminus at Maldon operated from 1848 until 1964. Typical of the latter-day trains was this Derby lightweight DMU photographed on 2 August 1959, although diesel railbuses were also seen on the branch. The extent of the station awning is particularly noteworthy.

The station site proved well worth a visit, but it was very difficult to get a corresponding picture! The track area is a vast timber yard; permission having been granted, I made my way between large stocks of wood to get a shot which included the Jacobean-type chimneys. A new brick building has been erected in front of the station, while the platform end extends into a narrow gully filled with old building materials and nettles. Curiously, the new bungalow is filled with an inner wall of breezeblocks. The station awning is still visible beyond the bungalow.
A.E. Bennett/DGS

KELVEDON: The Kelvedon signalman exchanges pleasantries with the crew of 'J15' 0-6-0 No 65443 as the loco drifts past the box on 6 April 1957. Two '50s-style enthusiasts look on.

Nowadays Kelvedon is very much an outer suburban station; with lengthened platforms, a new footbridge and modern buildings, the station bears little resemblance to its rural aspect of a quarter of a century earlier. The two other nondescript huts stand roughly where the signal box once dominated the scene. *R.C. Riley/RJA*

MARKS TEY: 'Britannia' 4-6-2 No 70041 *Sir John Moore* passes Marks Tey Yard signal box as it slows for the station stop with the 1.45 pm train from Norwich on Saturday 6 October 1956. Conveying through coaches from Melton Constable, this train was allowed 2 hours 55 minutes to cover the 115 miles from Norwich to London, inclusive of nine intermediate stops. In its way this was as much of a challenge to the loco and crew as was the later 2-hour 'Britannia' timing with only an Ipswich stop.

Thirty-five years later, the signal box is one of the few traditional boxes to remain on the Ipswich main line, whilst the semaphore signals controlling the sidings on the right are equally rare survivals. A Class '86' electric speeds south with a Norwich to London train, which in the 1990s is allowed 105 minutes for the journey, with four intermediate stops. (See also page 50) *R.C. Riley/RJA*

COLCHESTER: The Railway Enthusiasts Club 'Suffolk Venturer' railtour of 30 September 1956 pauses in the autumn sunshine at Colchester station behind spotless 'B12/3' 4-6-0 No 61576. The sharp curve through the platform, which necessitated a severe speed restriction for non-stopping trains, is particularly noticeable.

Colchester station presents a much changed face to the 1990s. A complete rebuilding in the early 1960s has eased the curves, enabling trains to run through at speed, whilst the modern lighting and trappings of electrification have altered the scene almost out of recognition. However, some of the former up platform buildings remain behind the modern facade, and the distinctive roof detail to the left can just be seen above the canopy in the 1956 picture.
.E. Bennett/RJA

COLCHESTER ST BOTOLPHS: Details such as the porters' barrows, the GER monogram on the seat, the ancient gas lamps and ornate spandrels all combine to give a traditional look to St Botolphs station at Colchester, despite the electric train at the platform. Somewhat unusually, the station is a terminus at the apex of a triangle, so that stopping trains have to reverse in order to continue their journey, while the third side of the triangle enables through trains to bypass the station.

In June 1991, nearly 32 years after the previous picture was taken, the structure of the station is little changed, although the awning has been cut back substantially. The station has now been renamed Colchester Town, in order to reflect its convenient position for the town centre. *A.E. Bennett/RJA*

WIVENHOE: The wait is over for passengers on the sharply curved platform as a 'B1' 4-6-0 pulls into Wivenhoe station with an up express on 2 August 1959. At this time the Clacton line was host to steam, diesel and electric traction, as the local service from Colchester had been electrified in the previous March, but there was still a gap in the wires between Colchester and Chelmsford. As a result, steam locomotives, gradually being replaced by the ever-growing fleet of main-line diesels, continued to handle the through trains to and from Liverpool Street, the so-called 'Clacton Interval Service', running roughly on an hourly basis during the day.

Wivenhoe station has changed little over the years, although the signal box has gone, and the former goods yard is now a car park. A Class '312' EMU heads for Walton-on-the-Naze on 21 June 1991. *A.E. Bennett/RJA*

BRIGHTLINGSEA: From 1866 until 1964 the little town of Brightlingsea, on the Essex marshes, was served by a 5-mile branch line from Wivenhoe. On 2 August 1959 a two-car Cravens diesel multiple unit waits at the terminus for its next 10-minute trip to the junction.

The branch survived heavy damage resulting from the 1953 floods, but the Beeching Report achieved what the forces of nature could not do, and the last train ran in June 1964. Brightlingsea Community Centre now stands on the site of the station, and a picture from the previous viewpoint would now only reveal the inside of a building. However, the house to the left links the two pictures, and the car is parked just about where the station building stood. Nearby, the Railway Tavern on the corner of Station Road reminds passers-by of what used to be. *A.E. Bennett/RJA*

THORPE-LE-SOKEN is where the Clacton line diverges from the line to Walton-on-the-Naze, which opened some 15 years earlier. For many years trains for the two coastal termini were combined and divided here, and 'B2' 4-6-0 No 1644 *Earlham Hall* was photographed joining the Clacton and Walton portions of an up train on 17 April 1949.

This procedure continued well into the electric era, but in the 1990s the pattern is for the Clacton and Walton trains to meet at Thorpe-le-Soken, with the former continuing fast to London, whilst the latter runs on to the capital as a semi-fast. In many cases the trains subsequently combine with services from Harwich and Braintree respectively. Following the departure of the Clacton train, a Class '312' electric unit forming the train from Walton leaves Thorpe-le-Soken on 21 June 1991. Only the island platform remains in use, and the goods yard, as at so many other places, is now a car park. *T.J. Edgington/RJA*

CLACTON: 'K1' 2-6-0 No 62069 stands at Clacton's platform 2 having arrived with a down train on 2 August 1959. Its train is formed of five coaches of five different types, to designs by Gresley, Thompson and British Railways. The fine selection of BR pictorial posters on the right and the scissors crossover for loco release are noteworthy.

Although the railway did not reach Clacton until comparatively late, in 1882, it carried heavy traffic as the town developed as a popular seaside resort and later as a London commuter area. However, in June 1991 contraction of the station facilities is evident — platform 3 has been demolished entirely, and the awnings on the surviving platforms have been cut back considerably. A Class '312' electric unit stands at the buffers. *A.E. Bennett/RJA*

HARWICH TOWN is an undistinguished structure at the back of the town; although occasional boat trains have penetrated this far, the prestigious continental traffic terminates $1^3/4$ miles short at Parkeston Quay. On 5 August 1959 a Cravens two-car diesel unit operating the branch service to Manningtree stands at the main platform, whilst a four-coach steam-hauled rake at the island platform forms the workmen's service to Parkeston Quay.

The branch was electrified in 1986, and as a result through services to London are now operated. Changes are evident at the main platform, where a Class '309' EMU has arrived from Liverpool Street on 21 June 1991, but the island platform has been demolished to simplify the loading of car flats with imported vehicles from the continent. *A.E. Bennett/RJA*

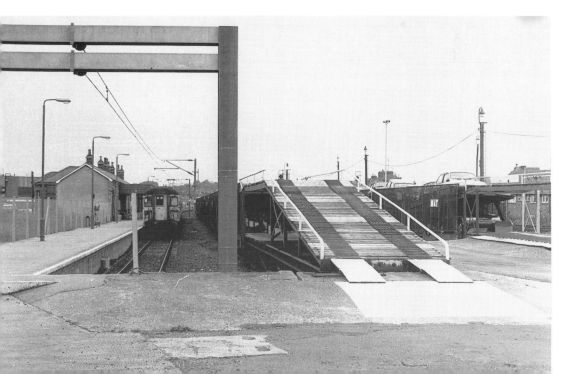

CAPEL: Bypassed by the main Ipswich line, the pleasant little town of Hadleigh was served by a branch from Bentley Junction which opened in 1847. Passenger traffic lasted for no more than 85 years, but the branch goods ran until 1965. The branch crossed the main A12 road by a level crossing next to Capel station. A combination of 'stop' sign, level crossing gates and flashing lights hold up road traffic as D5636 returns to the main line with the goods from Hadleigh. Only a Jaguar seems to be inconvenienced by its passing.

A quarter of a century later the road has become a dual carriageway, obliterating all trace of the former level crossing. The tree in the centre of the picture is, however, one of those seen behind the diesel in the earlier view. *H.N. James/RJA*

Towards the end of the branch's life, a Brush Type 2 diesel pauses while the train crew operate the gates over Hall Road, Bentley, close to a distinctively designed gatehouse. In 1991 the trackbed here is completely overgrown, frustrating any thought of a photograph from the same position. The gatehouse still stands, however, externally in good condition though empty and with no obvious means of approach. *H.N. James*

HADLEIGH: There is great concentration from the driver and shunter as D5699 moves a rake of wagons in an adjacent siding in Hadleigh yard with the aid of a chain attached to the coupling hook. This picture dates from the 1960s, when a daily goods train was still timetabled, and was allowed 2 hours to perform its duties at the branch terminus.

Eastwards from Hadleigh the line has become a public footpath, well signposted as the 'Hadleigh Railway Walk', which goes as far as the station at Raydon Wood. Young trees are now being grown where D5699 was shunting, while beyond the fence the immediate area of the station is firmly 'out of bounds'. Obscured by the bushes on the left, the station building itself is still standing, but securely boarded up. *H.N. James/RJA*

IPSWICH DOCKS were rail served on both sides of the River Orwell. On the west bank, a short branch from Halifax Junction ran to Griffin Wharf, serving engineering works and Ipswich Maltings. 'J15' 0-6-0 No 65459 potters around on typical 'dock line' track one sunny morning in the 1950s.

Rather surprisingly there are still rails on Griffin Wharf in the 1990s, serving as a headshunt for the West Bank Container terminal. In June 1991 Class '08' shunter No 08752 waits to propel empty freightliner flats into the terminal complex. Whilst the track layout has altered, the general atmosphere is not dissimilar. *Dr I.C. Allen/RJA*

IPSWICH: As the 1960s dawned, there were perhaps few finer sights on the railways of East Anglia than a shining Brunswick green 'Britannia' at the head of a rake of maroon BR Mark 1 coaches. No 70010 *Owen Glendower* is signalled away from the Ipswich stop with an up Norwich express on 8 September 1961, only a few days before the class was supplanted entirely by diesels on this service. *RJA*

The ubiquitous Brush Type 4 diesels, later to become Class '47', did not take over the London to Norwich service until 1965, and they remained the mainstay of the route until electrification in 1987. Here is the south end of Ipswich station with one of Stratford's fleet of silver-roofed Class '47s' waiting to leave with a London train in torrential rain in the early 1980s. Colour light signals and standard BR black and white signs have arrived on the scene. *A.C. Ingram*

Together with the other boxes in the area, Ipswich station signal box was demolished in 1984, thus providing a clear sight of the tunnel mouth from this viewpoint. Class '86' No 86232 *Norwich Festival* waits to leave for London on a dull June day in 1991, as a down express, driven from the leading DBSO and with the loco at the rear, emerges from the tunnel. *RJA*

Byways on the Suffolk/Essex border

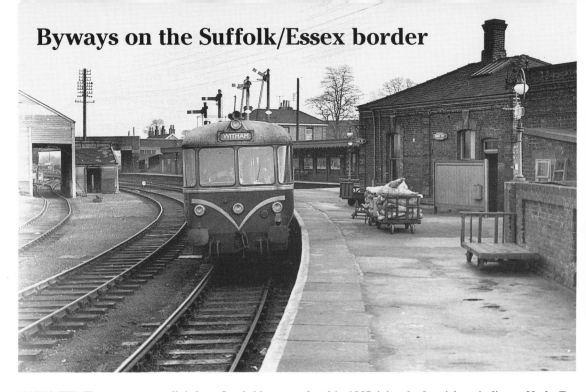

MARKS TEY: The cross-country link from Cambridge, completed in 1865, joins the Ipswich main line at Marks Tey (see also page 38). The branch has its own sharply curving platform face as it turns west from the main line. Regardless of the destination blind, this four-wheeled railbus, built by the German firm of Waggon Maschinenbau , is bound for Haverhill via the Colne Valley route, as it awaits departure time on 21 November 1959. These railbuses were widely used on the lightly loaded services in the area.

A two-car Class '101' diesel unit stands at the same spot with the branch train for Sudbury in 1991 — at least nobody will be misled by the destination blind! The goods shed is in private use, the main line has been resignalled and electrified, and the yard, inevitably, has become a car park. However, the 'feel' of the branch platform has changed little over the years, and at how many other places on BR today can one find a branch-line train standing at a rural junction awaiting the main-line connection? *A.E. Bennett/RJA*

CHAPPEL & WAKES COLNE: There can be no doubt as to the location of this picture as 'E4' 2-4-0 No 62788, the predecessor of the railbus opposite, heads the 5.30 train from Sudbury to Marks Tey on 15 April 1949. The coaches are of North Eastern, LNER and Great Central vintage — a not untypical combination at the time. Chappel & Wakes Colne was the junction for the independent Colne Valley & Halstead Railway, giving a more direct route to Haverhill from 1860 onwards.

Since the 1970s the station has been the home of a preservation centre, now the East Anglian Railway Museum. The original goods shed and yard hut still stand amongst the railway artifacts in the background, as a diesel unit arrives from Sudbury. The inspiration for the replacement nameboard is obvious! *T.J. Edgington/RJA*

HALSTEAD: The Colne Valley & Halstead Railway retained its independence until the Grouping, and the line survived as an alternative route from Chappel to Haverhill until the end of 1961. On 10 August 1958, 'J15' 0-6-0 No 65440 poses for the cameras at Halstead whilst working the REC 'Northern and Eastern' railtour.

I needed some local help here to identify the exact position, as a garage now occupies the station site, but the top of the goods shed with its rounded window is visible on the right. Across the road the nearby Tortoise Iron Foundry is now derelict. A dispute in 1900 between the railway company and the foundry over a siding resulted in much bad feeling and a wall, known as the 'spite wall', was built in front of the Foundry Manager's house. *A.E. Bennett/DGS*

SUDBURY: The first railway to Sudbury, from Marks Tey, opened to a town centre terminus in 1849, but when the line from Cambridge and Haverhill reached the town 13 years later it was necessary to build a new station on the sharp curve connecting the two routes. The original station continued in use as a goods depot. On 9 June 1956, its final day in traffic, 'E4' 2-4-0 No 62792 is signalled away from Sudbury with a train from Cambridge. Beyond the station footbridge, a second footbridge carries a public right of way over the line.

Following the withdrawal of services to the west in 1967, Sudbury became a terminus once more, and the unstaffed station rapidly degenerated to a vandalised ruin. More recently, Network SouthEast has provided a smart new platform. Framed by the footpath bridge, a Class '101' DMU appears round the corner towards the new platform on 10 May 1991. The angle of the footbridge steps in relation to the running line shows the altered position of the platform, whilst the car park on the right is on the site of the second station. *R.C. Riley/DGS*

LONG MELFORD: Seen from the station footbridge, ex-GNR 'C12' 4-4-2T No 67367 runs round its train for Bury St Edmunds on 2 April 1956. Beyond the signal box, the Bury line curves to the right, whilst the 'main line' to Cambridge veers to the left. It is interesting to note that in 1871 Bury could be reached from Liverpool Street in $2^3/_4$ hours via Marks Tey and Melford (renamed Long Melford later); there were four trains each way on the branch on weekdays, but no Sunday service.

Like many other stations in this area, Long Melford's finest hours were during the Second World War, but today the station house has a 'For Sale' board outside, and a pool occupies part of the trackbed. *T.J. Edgington/DGS*

LAVENHAM: The layout of the goods yard at Lavenham, the first station down the Bury line, could provide interesting inspiration for the space-starved modeller! The train at the platform is the special 'last train' of 4 June 1961, normal passenger services having been withdrawn some eight weeks previously in April. A few wagons are dotted around the yard, as Lavenham was to survive as the terminus of a goods line from Bury St Edmunds for another four years.

The area is now covered by warehouses, but the station chimneys are just visible by the further road bridge and the church still looks down on the scene as the mode of transport has changed over the years. *A.E. Bennett/DGS*

COCKFIELD: The special 'last train' of 4 June 1961 behind a Brush Type 2 diesel, with a less-than-ornate headboard brings unprecedented custom to the next station down the line, the single platform at Cockfield.

Extensively used by American servicemen during the Second World War, the rural lanes were once busy with military transport collecting new arrivals for the local air bases. In the spring of 1991 the old station slumbers in the bright sunshine, deserted and semi-derelict. Most old stations, if not swept away, have been put to some use, residential or commercial, but Cockfield appears to be one of the exceptions. *A.E. Bennett/DGS*

CLARE: On the other branch from Long Melford, a two-car Cravens DMU set runs into a deserted Clare station on 5 September 1960. According to the destination blind, it will finish its journey at Haverhill.

Clare closed to goods in October 1966 and to passengers in March 1967, and probably one of the nicest ways for a railway station to spend its retirement is, as here, in a country park setting. The building serves as the Warden's home, the trackbed and surrounding area are lawned and a length of track enters the old goods shed; inside is a van with many facts and figures regarding the station and the Stour Valley railway in general. *D. Thompson/DGS*

HAVERHILL: During the 1950s the ancient ex-GER power on the branches in the Cambridge area was supplemented by lightweight Ivatt '2MT' 2-6-0s of LMSR design. One of these, No 46466, is seen passing Haverhill Junction on 27 May 1957, the signal indicating that it is bound for the Colne Valley line via Halstead. The tender cabs were no doubt much appreciated by the crews when running tender-first, as previously only a tarpaulin draped over the cab had protected them from the elements.

Up a short thoroughfare bearing the old title Station Road one comes to the site of Haverhill station today, platform edges still discernible under the weeds and the roofs of the sheds in the earlier picture still visible; it is most noticeable that it has been realised that these old goods sheds were so well built that in many cases they can still be put to good use today. To the east the three-arched Hamlet Road viaduct linking the Colne Valley and GER lines remains and is the subject of a preservation order; when we visited the town a large banner was unfurled over the parapet congratulating someone on their 40th birthday. *R.M. Casserley/DGS*

SAFFRON WALDEN: Ex-GER Class 'E4' 2-4-0 No 62787 pauses at Saffron Walden in the summer of 1956 with a local train from Audley End to Bartlow (see 'Past & Present' No 10). Steam trains, often a push-pull set, were later replaced by four-wheel diesel railbuses, but even these could not save the line, closure coming in September 1964.

Up a hill at the top of the town and looking down from the bridge, we found the building practically derelict and new vans parked on the platform and trackbed; beyond there is a car-wash and garage. A local inhabitant told me that the station building is owned by an adjoining garage and is in the process of being converted into flats, so its life is assured for a number of years yet. *R.C. Riley/DGS*

East Suffolk line and branches

IPSWICH: Proudly bearing express passenger headcode discs, 'D16/3' 4-4-0 No 62597 of Yarmouth South Town shed (32D) pulls into Ipswich in June 1956. It is no doubt bound for its home station via the East Suffolk line.

Ipswich station has survived electrification rather better than many others, and the awnings remain a distinctive feature. A general cleaning up of the station buildings is also evident as Class '37' No 37219 heads a single engineers 'Tench' wagon north over much simplified trackwork. *R.C. Riley/RJA*

ORWELL: The 'L1' 2-6-4Ts from Ipswich depot were staple power for the Felixstowe branch in the last decade of steam working. No 67709 drifts into Orwell station with an up train on 7 October 1956.

Sunshine and shadow on a wooded section of the Felixstowe line. . . but two pillars appear in a gap in the trees to the right, giving a clue that this photograph was taken from virtually the same spot as the previous one. Orwell station closed in 1959, and although the platforms and loop were soon removed, the platform building still stands, almost hidden from the railway. *R.C. Riley/RJA*

FELIXSTOWE TOWN: Although the Felixstowe line opened in 1877, it was not until 21 years later that the terminus at Felixstowe Town was opened. A spacious station, with four platform faces, it handled heavy traffic in the summer, and all trains continuing to Felixstowe Beach and the docks had to reverse there. The generous facilities are well shown in this photograph of 'L1' 2-6-4T No 67710 awaiting departure time on 5 August 1959. *A.E. Bennett*

With the upsurge of goods traffic to the Port of Felixstowe in the 1970s, the reversal procedure became too time-consuming, so the original 1877 line was re-opened, avoiding Felixstowe Town. Staff were withdrawn, and the facilities were reduced to the bare minimum needed to handle the diesel unit shuttling to and from Ipswich. Rapidly the whole place fell into a state of decay. *D.C. Pearce*

By the 'eighties, the town centre site was too valuable to leave derelict, and the redundant land was sold off. The line now terminates half-way down the platform, but the truncated remains of the awning still provide shelter for passengers. A Texas store stands on the site of the goods yard, while the station building houses a shopping centre, with plenty of car parking available. *RJA*

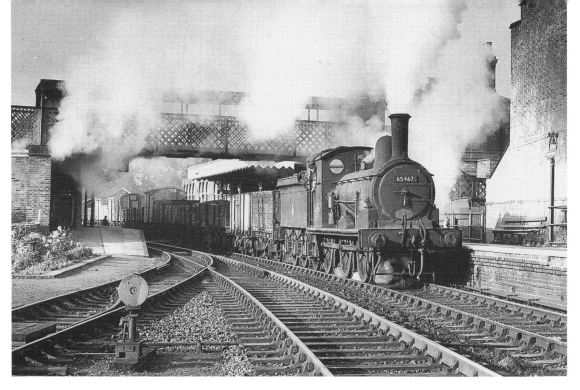

WOODBRIDGE: Despite their diminutive appearance, the GER-design 'J15' 0-6-0s were powerful little machines, and No 65467 is coping well with a substantial load as it passes Woodbridge with the Ipswich to Framlingham pick-up on 10 October 1957.

Woodbridge station has worn the years well, retaining a prosperous air with its double track and footbridge. The station buildings serve as a restaurant, and the canopies survive, although the stinging nettles and fence are a poor substitute for the Great Eastern ground signal. The inevitable radio-fitted Class '101' unit is about to move on to the single track section northwards to Saxmundham. *R.C. Riley/RJA*

WICKHAM MARKET: 'J15' 0-6-0 No 65389 is seen at Wickham Market station in May 1957, during the course of a diagram covering the freight workings on both the Framlingham and Snape branches. The cattle wagons are a reminder of an important traffic in this predominantly rural area, while the sidings, double track main line and imposing signal box all add to the impression of a busy railway location.

Together with all the other East Suffolk line stations, Wickham Market became an unstaffed halt in March 1967, and the line between Woodbridge and Saxmundham was singled as part of the economies carried out in the mid-1980s. In 1991 the station building is still in a good state of repair, being used as an antiques showroom, although the awning has gone, to be replaced by a 'bus stop'-type shelter, and only the former down platform is still in use. An aerial in connection with the radio signalling stands, no doubt coincidentally, where the signal box once controlled the passing traffic. The line does, however, still provide a useful social service, as three passengers watch the arrival of an early afternoon train for Ipswich on 20 June 1991. *R.C. Riley/RJA*

MARLESFORD: The branch line from Wickham Market to Framlingham opened in 1859, and a sparse passenger service survived for 93 years. The goods traffic lingered on until Easter 1965, although by the early 'sixties the Working Timetable shows the train to be running on Mondays, Wednesdays and Fridays only. In its final years, the branch goods was allowed an hour to cover the 6 miles 37 chains from Wickham Market to Framlingham. This generous schedule was partly due to the need for the train crew to operate the several sets of level crossing gates on the line, including this set over a very minor road just 270 yards west of the A12 level crossing by Marlesford station. Even in passenger days certain of the crossing gates were worked by the train crew, and this picture shows the time-honoured ritual being enacted during the last days of the branch. The station building at Marlesford can be seen immediately to the left of the loco cab.

In 1991 the course of the railway can be followed clearly across the field in the foreground as it heads for the distant Marlesford station. The boundary fence remains, as does part of the fencing by the level crossing, and in this very rural part of Suffolk there is little change to the buildings along the line of the main road in the background. Owing to development across the trackbed behind the photographer, the photograph had to be taken from the road at the point where it crosses the railway. *H.N. James/RJA*

SAXMUNDHAM: 'Britannia' 'Pacific' No 70030 *William Wordsworth* moves an up express away from Saxmundham past the tall starter signal, on 5 August 1959.

In the spring of 1991 a Class '101' diesel unit pauses at a still neat and tidy Saxmundham station. The 1959 view cannot be duplicated exactly as the staggered down platform from which it was taken is now abandoned, a new one having been built on the site of the goods yard opposite the up platform. The footbridge, crossover, and goods yard have gone, but the signal box is still there, acting as the control centre for the line's radio signalling. In the 1990s the radio aerial and automatic crossing barriers point skywards, as did the signal, loco exhaust and telegraph pole a generation earlier. *A.E. Bennett/RJA*

LEISTON: The branch from Saxmundham to Leiston opened in 1859, and the extension to Aldeburgh followed the next year. Leiston was the home of the well-known engineering firm of Richard Garrett, whose extensive premises were rail-connected. Until 1962 their private siding was the haunt of the distinctive Aveling & Porter geared loco *Sirapite* which is seen here at Leiston station in October 1956, dwarfed by a 16-ton mineral wagon.

Following closure to passengers in 1966, the line survived as far as Sizewell, a mile or so beyond Leiston, for traffic in connection with Sizewell power station, and there has been an upsurge of traffic with recent new construction. Leiston station building is now in use as a dwelling, with the TV satellite dish providing a sign of the times, whilst the former goods shed, to the left of the picture, has also been converted to residential use. The sidings where *Sirapite* once shunted are now overgrown by trees, and the one remaining track looks neglected.
R.C. Riley/RJA

ALDEBURGH: With its overall roof the station at Aldeburgh epitomised the branch-line terminus. By the time this first picture was taken in August 1959 a two-car Cravens DMU resplendent in its green livery had replaced the former ancient steam loco and two coaches. Nevertheless, the gas lamps, barrows and blue 'totem' signs not to mention the small boy 'chatting up' the driver, are all part of the traditional scene. *A.E Bennett*

During the last few months before closure, the station lost its overall roof, and this photograph from the late 'sixties shows a sad scene of decay after the tracks had been lifted. By revealing the houses facing the railway, it does however provide a useful link with the third picture. *Lens of Sutton*

In the summer of 1991 the station yard has vanished completely under a housing estate, whose gardens are shielded from the road by the wall on the extreme right. A new road, leading to further housing development cuts diagonally across the site of the platform and buildings. *RJA*

HALESWORTH: Once the junction for the 3-foot gauge Southwold Railway, Halesworth remained a busy freight centre until the early 'sixties, and traffic from the up and down yards and thriving milk depot justified the provision of a shunting engine sent light daily from Lowestoft. Evidence of the buoyant traffic is all around on 3 May 1958 as 'J39' 0-6-0 No 64826, an Ipswich engine, busies itself in the down yard.

Within five years the whole East Suffolk line was to be under threat from the Beeching Report; within a decade all the sidings would be removed and the goods traffic would be gone for ever. In 1991 the site of the down yard is in industrial use, and the up yard has disappeared under a housing development. A three-car DMU heads for Ipswich, and it is only the drain cover in the right foreground of each picture which provides the link between the two. *R.C. Riley/RJA*

Halesworth signal box became redundant with the advent of radio signalling on the line but was preserved thanks to the efforts of a group of local enthusiasts. It was moved to the grounds of a nearby school, where it now stands as a delightful reminder of bygone days. *RJA*

BECCLES: A 'B1' 4-6-0 pauses in the winter sunshine at Beccles with a down passenger train on 28 February 1959. As the signals indicate, Beccles was a three-way junction, with the Waveney Valley line branching to the left, the direct line to Yarmouth via Haddiscoe continuing straight on, and the Lowestoft line diverging to the right. Behind the running-in board is the substantial locomotive shed.

A radio-fitted three-car Class '101' DMU arrives at Beccles, which has suffered more than any other station as a result of the 1980s rationalisation of the East Suffolk line. Only a single track to Lowestoft threads the once busy area, although there is local pressure to install a passing loop to improve line capacity and flexibility of working. The island platform is no longer used and the building has been demolished, its site being indicated by a large clump of weeds. Trees have engulfed the area behind the island platform, obliterating any view of the loco shed building, which is still standing. *A.E. Bennett/RJA*

BUNGAY: The Waveney Valley line was one of those typically East Anglian cross-country branches connecting the north-to-south trunk routes. Opened in stages between 1855 and 1863, it connected Beccles on the East Suffolk line with Tivetshall on the Ipswich to Norwich route (see page 81), and the sparse passenger service was withdrawn in 1953. Three years later, Bungay station is still neat and tidy as 'J15' 0-6-0 No 65447 waits for its trainload of enthusiasts to rejoin the Railway Enthusiasts Club special train on 30 September 1956. *H.C. Casserley*

As the line opened in stages, so it closed. Freight traffic was withdrawn from the central Bungay to Harleston section in 1960, from Harleston to Tivetshall in 1966, from Bungay to Ditchingham, the next station east, in 1964, and the surviving eastern stub a year later. For many years Bungay station remained derelict, but eventually the trackbed was utilised for the construction of a much needed bypass for the town. *D.C. Pearce*

Following the opening of the new road in 1983, little remains to indicate that the station ever existed. The arched bridge carrying a minor road over the railway has been replaced by a modern design, but the sleeper-built hut on the right is of obviously 'railway' origin, and the houses behind it are common to both the 1956 and 1991 views. *JA*

YARMOUTH SOUTH TOWN: Looking at the reduced railway scene of the 1990s, it is often difficult to recall just how much land even a medium-sized station could take up. This is well illustrated by this view of the approach to Yarmouth South Town, seen from a down 'B1'-hauled train in February 1959.

Once the terminus of London expresses, South Town declined in importance during the 1960s, and the surviving 'pay train' service to Lowestoft was withdrawn in 1970. Inevitably, the central site soon disappeared underneath new roads, superstores and industrial units, and the previous viewpoint can no longer be used. However, the buildings on the right appear in the earlier picture, and the distinctive town hall clock-tower remains on the skyline. *A.E. Bennett/RJA*

North and West from Ipswich

HAUGHLEY JUNCTION (1): The headcode reveals that this up train passing Haughley Junction signal box behind a 'K3' 2-6-0 is in fact an empty stock working. To the left, the line to Bury St Edmunds trails in behind the signal box, whilst the single track to the right is the Mid Suffolk Light Railway to Laxfield (see page 75), climbing steadily away from the main line at a gradient of 1 in 42.

On a June evening in 1991, Class '86' No 86215 *Joseph Chamberlain* sweeps down Haughley bank with an up Norwich express. The signals and box have gone, and a ladder junction controlled from Colchester power box has simplified the trackwork of the diverging line to Bury. Of the Mid Suffolk there is no trace, the whole area being lost beneath bushes and young trees. *Dr I.C. Allen/RJA*

HAUGHLEY JUNCTION (2): An up stopping train headed by 'B12/3' 4-6-0 No 61580 moves away from Haughley Junction station on 3 May 1958. Not much effort is needed to get the short train under way on the downhill stretch to the next stop at Stowmarket.

Since the last passenger train called at the end of 1966, Haughley Junction station buildings and platform have been largely demolished. The granary continues to survey the few sad remains on 19 June 1991. *R.C. Riley/RJA*

LAXFIELD: No coverage of East Anglian railways would be complete without a mention of the Mid Suffolk Light Railway. An independent company from its opening in 1904 until the LNER took over, the 19-mile line from Haughley Junction was only part of an ambitious plan for a network of light railways across mid-Suffolk, but the rails had only reached a mile or so beyond Laxfield when the money ran out. Laxfield terminus is seen here on 18 April 1949 with 'J15' 0-6-0 No 5459 heading two of the six-wheeled coaches which provided the passenger accommodation almost to the end.

It was no surprise when the last train ran on the Mid Suffolk in 1952 — the surprise was that the line had lasted so long. By its very 'light railway' nature, there were few earthworks and the stations were basic structures, so few relics of the line can be found today. At Laxfield the platform is a barely discernable grass-grown mound, and only a rotting gate in the hedgerow provides a clue to the site, so for the contrasting picture we show the scene in 1959. Although the track has gone, the station buildings are still intact after seven years of disuse; the days when derelict buildings become targets for vandals and aerosol paint sprays are still in the future! *T.J. Edgington/RJA*

BURY ST EDMUNDS: In June 1960 an ex-LNER Class 'K3' 2-6-0 prepares to leave Bury St Edmunds. The express passenger headcode and destination boards on certain of the coaches would appear to suggest that the train is one of the cross-country boat trains from the North West to Harwich.

Where the 'K3' stood, 31 years later an Anglia Region two-car DMU, No L223, pulls away on a Cambridge to Ipswich train. It is a refreshing change to see goods yards still active, with a Class '37' and Class '08' shunters busy with hopper wagons in the distance. The station, built in a grand style, boasts a newsagent, subterranean booking hall, and subway to platforms 1 and 2, but as is so often the case these days, the two middle tracks through the station have vanished; I was accompanied to a spot to get an identical view matching yesteryear's photograph. *R.C. Riley/DGS*

SAXHAM & RISBY: A passenger and the porter watch as a stopping train pulls into Saxham & Risby station on the Bury–Newmarket line in the summer of 1937. Not surprisingly, the loco is one of the ex-GER 'E4' 2-4-0s which handled so much of this kind of traffic at the time.

I found it impossible to get an identical shot here; the platform from which the previous picture was taken has ceased to exist. The station building behind me on the up side still stands, in a poor condition, but the former platform is a wired-off car park in an industrial complex. At least the road bridge is still visible in both photographs, as a Class '158' speeds towards Newmarket. *D. Thompson/DGS*

NEWMARKET: Five coaches of five different designs behind a 'D16/3' 4-4-0 form a typical local train of the period as No 62609 waits to head east from Newmarket on 19 September 1953. Newmarket station, with its lengthy canopies, was far from typical, though. The lavish facilities were, of course, provided to cope with the traffic handled on race days, when even Pullman car trains from London used to terminate here.

Thirty-eight years later Anglian Region DMU No L223 pulls into Newmarket station on a Cambridge train. The old station buildings are wired off along most of the platform, leaving a narrow ledge to walk along, although the east end of the platform is still full width with a couple of 'bus shelters'. It was impossible to match the picture with that of yesteryear, both the second track and platform having vanished. *H.C. Casserley/DGS*

DISS: 'History begins yesterday', they say, and certainly this is the case at Diss. The northern approach to the station had a distinctly traditional look about it as recently as 1 September 1984, with complicated trackwork and even a 16-ton mineral wagon standing on a grass-grown siding. Class '47' No 47587 is approaching with the 12.32 from Norwich to Liverpool Street.

Just seven years later the main line has been electrified and things have been tidied up considerably. The trackwork has been simplified, although the kink in the remaining siding remains from the earlier scene. The jumble of buildings in the goods yard has been swept away, and a 'pay and display' car park has replaced the previous haphazard parking amongst the huts. Class '86' No 86220 *Round Tabler* approaches the station with a typical up express of the 'nineties. *D.C. Pearce/RJA*

BURSTON: Following their introduction in 1958, the English Electric Type 4 diesels, later known as Class '40', began to oust the 'Britannia' 'Pacifics' from the Ipswich main line expresses. D206, however, is on a far more mundane duty as it pulls into Burston station with the 6.08 pm stopping train from Norwich to Ipswich on 27 June 1964. Only one of the four vehicles appears to have passenger accommodation, and the Gresley full brake at the front contrasts with the modern diesel.

In common with the other wayside village stations on the route, Burston closed in November 1966, and the platforms were later demolished. The station building, which replaced an older structure between the wars, is still used by a local furniture maker, and the different coloured brickwork reveals where the poster boards used to be. The main line has of course been electrified, and the area is now controlled by Colchester power box. *Both RJA*

TIVETSHALL: Until January 1953 passengers could change at Tivetshall for the Waveney Valley branch train to Beccles (see pages 70-1). Although both the branch and the station closed completely in 1966, the signal box, refuge loop and some of the sidings survived for another 20 years. No 47583 *County of Hertfordshire* passes the box with the 9.30 am from Liverpool Street to Norwich on 1 September 1984, while an engineers vehicle stands on the surviving stub of the Waveney Valley branch.

The whole line to Norwich is now controlled by Colchester power box, and Tivetshall box was demolished soon after becoming redundant; the sidings and loop were removed at the same time. With the inelegant DBSO leading, a down express passes the site of Tivetshall box in August 1991. The concrete ballast bin on the right has survived the changes, whilst a yellow BR van shows that the railway still has some interest in the former yard area.
P.C. Pearce/RJA

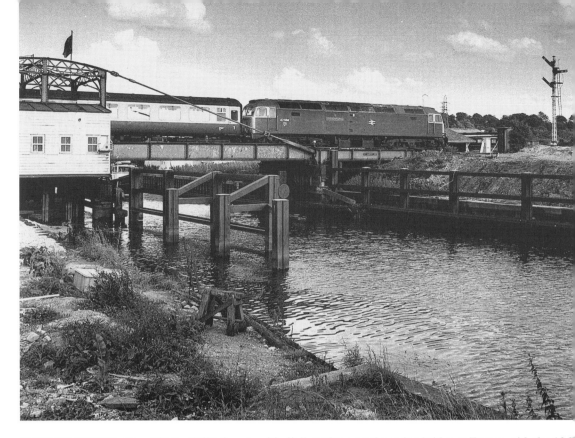

NORWICH TROWSE: Class '47' No 47584 *County of Suffolk* rattles over the swing bridge at Trowse with the 16.3█ from Norwich to Liverpool Street on 25 August 1985. By this time the structure was some 80 years old and in urge█ need of replacement. The signal post, with arms controlling traffic in both directions, is worthy of note.

The extension of electrification to Norwich provided the opportunity to replace the bridge, with its 15 mph spee█ restriction, and a new bridge was built a few yards upstream, coming into use in February 1987. Electric current i█ carried over the swinging section of the new single-line bridge by means of a fixed overhead bar which connec█ with the catenary wires at each end of the bridge. The fixed overhead is clearly seen in this picture, as Class '86' N█ 86232 *Norwich Festival* propels the 13.30 Liverpool Street–Norwich on the last leg of its journey on 5 August 199█ *Both D.C. Pearce*

NORWICH VICTORIA: In the immediate post-war years Victoria station was completely re-organised and claimed to possess the country's most up-to-date goods yards. Storage for about 500 wagons of coal and other merchandise was needed daily at Norwich rail depots and the new yard gave much needed relief to Thorpe. Victoria station had not been used as a passenger station since 1916, although it was used as a coal concentration depot until 1986.

The area has since suffered the same fate as so many former railway yards, namely a supermarket complex and a car park. The building to the left of the three-arch road bridge is, however, still clearly visible today. *Norfolk Railway Society Archive/DGS*

Great Eastern lines in Norfolk

NORWICH DEPOT: The final steam locomotive to be allocated to Norwich Depot was fittingly an ex-GER design, 'J17' 0-6-0 No 65567. Framed in the sand hopper, it potters around in Norwich shed yard on 25 March 1962, less than a week before being transferred away. Brush Type 2 No D5567 stands in front of the soon-to-be redundant coaling tower, whilst two BTH Type 1s of the D82XX series are also present. *RJA*

The coaling tower was demolished soon afterwards, and the site was taken over by Charringtons, the fuel distributors. However, the sand hopper road remained as a headshunt for Norwich loco shed until it was superseded by the new traction maintenance depot at Crown Point in 1983. A Class '37' stands under the sander adjacent to the oil depot whilst a sister locomotive stands outside the running shed. The line of buildings on the left in front of the water tank at one time contained the District Mechanical Engineer's Office and an ambulance room. The 'dods' are off for the '37' to reverse towards the station on 6 April 1977. *D.C. Pearce*

By May 1991 the loco depot site was derelict, but the old hopper still stood, framing two of Norwich's allocation of Class '08' diesel shunters. *RJA*

BUCKENHAM opened with the Yarmouth & Norwich Railway in 1844; 120 years later, a Metro-Cammell DMU smokes away towards Norwich, passing a nicely contrasting pair of signals.

Serving a scattered marshland community, it is remarkable that Buckenham station remains open today, although only one train a day in each direction is booked to call there in the 1991 summer timetable. The signals have gone, although the box survived until the late 1980s, and the station building is now in residential use. Class '86' electric No 86208 *City of Chester* is an unlikely visitor some 8 miles from the nearest catenary. Following the introduction of pull-push working between Norwich and London, the trains have been regarded as semi-fixed formations and in summer, when certain of these workings run through to Yarmouth, the electric loco is dragged to the coast and back to obviate the need for extra shunting at Norwich station. *A.E. Bennett/RJA*

YARMOUTH VAUXHALL: Having arrived from Norwich, 'D16/3' 4-4-0 No 62511 simmers at Yarmouth's Vauxhall terminus on a somewhat damp 31 August 1958. The unattended suitcase is a sign of more relaxed times — in the 1990s it would probably cause an evacuation of the entire area!

In July 1991 an elderly DMU set stands at the spot where No 62511 stood in 1958. Almost isolated in a sea of seemingly never-ending road traffic, Yarmouth's surviving railway station stands adjacent to the Asda superstore; very matter-of-fact with no frills, as befits today's railway, there is none the less a good-sized forecourt even including a bookstall with the old words 'W.H.Smith & Son' discernable under the new name. The platforms curve away to the left with signal box and semaphore starter signals at the platform end, rusty sidings to the right and just beyond the station the tracks with walkways intact which formed the extensive coach sidings of past years. The station canopy has been removed back to the buffer stops and forecourt. *A.E. Bennett/DGS*

YARMOUTH QUAYSIDE TRAMWAY: The tramway from Yarmouth Vauxhall to the quayside was for a few years the home of the 'Y10' 0-4-0 double-ended Sentinel locomotives, originally used on the Wisbech & Upwell line. With the crew keeping a sharp lookout, No 8186 makes its way along Hall Quay with a goods train from the docks. The 'NE' lettering dates this scene in the late '40s/early '50s.

Forty years on, the facades of the buildings on Hall Quay are largely unchanged, but motorists no longer need fear the passage of a lengthy goods train. The complicated one-way system is, however, perhaps an even greater hazard. *Dr I.C. Allen/RJA*

CROMER HIGH: 'B1' 4-6-0 No 61051 pulls out of the original GER terminus at Cromer, before passenger services were concentrated on Cromer Beach station in 1954. Goods trains continued to use the yard until 1960, after which the site stood derelict for some years.

I climbed up a steep embankment to reach this site and walked between stacks of bricks towards the parapet of the old bridge. New houses are being built on the site, and there is easier access to the area from the Norwich road, this being not the most convenient site for a station, on an escarpment overlooking and about a mile from the town centre. Here the M&GN scored with their Beach station, in a more favourable position near the town. A few hundred yards to the south-east of this spot the Norfolk & Suffolk joint line ran under the GE on its way north-westwards to join the M&GN line at Runton West Junction (see page 112). I am standing where the telegraph pole was in the earlier picture; had I stepped back I would have fallen into the road, the bridge having long since gone!
M&GN Circle, E. Tuddenham/DGS

COLTISHALL: With a load of concrete beams from Lenwade, train 7Z61 passes the remains of Coltishall station on the branch from Wroxham to County School on 4 June 1968. Brush Type 2 No D5563 double-heads its blue-painted sister No D5545, a combination required for braking rather than haulage capacity. Freight traffic over this route declined during the 'seventies, and the line closed to all traffic in 1982.

Eight years later, the railway from Wroxham to Aylsham reopened, albeit on 15-inch gauge track. Although a new platform and passing loop have been built beyond the original platform end, the old station building at Coltishall has changed but little. A Bure Valley Railway train is negotiating the spring points out of the loop as it heads towards Wroxham behind loco No 24. Formerly on the Fairbourne Railway, No 24 was regauged and moved to Norfolk in the early summer of 1991. *Both RJA*

THEMELTHORPE: Early in the BR era, a 'J17' 0-6-0 heads a lengthy cattle train along the GE line and under the girder bridge carrying the M&GN at Themelthorpe. The two railways also crossed at Fakenham but there the M&GN passed beneath the Great Eastern. The railwayman posing on the bridge could indicate that a special stop was made in the middle of the section to enable this picture to be taken. Could such an irregularity have taken place? Headquarters was certainly many miles away from this remote spot!

Standing in the stubble of a field on a hot late summer's day in 1990 looking at the remains of a railway bridge, it was hard to visualize that two railways crossed at this point. The embankment on either side of the bridge has been cut away to allow tractor access into the fields on each side of the cutting. A few hundred yards to the east is the trackbed of the Themelthorpe Curve, opened in 1960 to avoid a lengthy round trip of some 64 miles to points only a mile apart, Norwich's former City and Thorpe stations. *M&GN Circle, E. Tuddenham/DGS*

FOULSHAM, the last station on the branch before the junction at County School, looking east back towards Aylsham. In the early years of this century the station saw nine trains a day, and the Second World War revived its fortunes, as with many other stations near RAF bases, but this activity was wound down during the 'fifties, the station closing in October 1964.

Foulsham station today is in private occupation, and the present owners were very cooperative, showing my wife and I photographs of the station in its heyday. They produce honey and the air is heavy with a sweet smell and the bustle of bees. *M&GN Circle, E. Tuddenham/DGS*

COUNTY SCHOOL: The headcode disc shows that 'D1' 4-4-0 No 3062, a GNR design introduced to the area by the LNER, is heading a train from the Wroxham branch as it pulls into the station at County School soon after the Second World War. Only the station dog provides any sign of life. The single lines from Wells and Wroxham converged at a point a mile or so north of County School, and ran independently, each with its own set of mileposts, to the station. Most trains ran through to Dereham or beyond, so the terminal and run-round facilities at the outer face of the island platform on the right of the picture were rarely used. Nevertheless, the station retained a rural junction atmosphere, if not its collection of enamel signs, right up to the withdrawal of passenger trains in October 1964.

Goods trains continued to run through the increasingly neglected station for many years, but by the mid-1980s even this traffic had gone, and the tracks were torn up. More recently, however, the station has become the headquarters of the Fakenham & Dereham Railway Society, who have made commendable progress in restoring the area. *D. Thompson/DGS*

DEREHAM: With the Norwich to Wells line going north, and the Kings Lynn line running west, Dereham was a busy country junction in its time. As the lines converged facing the Wells direction, passenger trains between Norwich and Kings Lynn had to reverse in the station, although there was an avoiding line used by freight and excursion traffic not needing to call at Dereham. The complex was controlled by no fewer than four signal boxes, Dereham North, South, West and, rather spoiling the geographical completeness, Central. It is the imposing Central box which dominates the scene as Brush Type 2 No D5661 shunts the daily Fakenham goods in the busy yard on 30 May 1969. Although by now passenger services to both north and west had been withdrawn, the passenger trains to Norwich would continue to run for another four months, whilst regular freight traffic was to continue until the end of the 1980s.

Following the closure of the Wells line to passenger trains in 1964, the freight service was cut back first to Fakenham, and then progressively to Ryburgh and North Elmham as traffic declined. Latterly little used, the line from Wymondham to Dereham itself closed entirely in 1989, and is now the subject of an ambitious preservation scheme. A company called the Great Eastern Co has been formed and is working to provide a service to Wymondham, using mixed steam and diesel. The track down to Wymondham, some 11 miles away, is still in position, which is a bonus. In the summer of 1991, however, the remaining tracks at Dereham are in a state of limbo, awaiting an uncertain future. *RJA/DGS*

RYBURGH: Unlike the other lines to the North Norfolk coast, the Wells line was not swamped with heavy weekend excursion traffic. Those specials which did run were often for the benefit of pilgrims visiting the shrines at Walsingham, and one such train travels through typical mid-Norfolk countryside just south of Ryburgh station on 16 August 1959, with 'D16/3' 4-4-0 No 62544 at the head of nine corridor coaches. On the far horizon is the water tower on the Sennowe Park estate.

To find this spot today one must take an obscure unclassified road which runs roughly parallel and to the west of the A1067, and beneath a road bridge one finds the usual signs of a defunct railway, post-and-wire fencing and linear scrub, although, of course, this line was closed only comparatively recently. The water tower in the previous picture is just visible again on the horizon. *M&GN Circle, E. Tuddenham/DGS*

FAKENHAM EAST: The station at Fakenham remained substantially intact following the withdrawal of passenger trains in 1964, although inevitably there was some rationalisation of the trackwork. This was the scene on 21 April 1979 when the station hosted the 'Fakenham Flyer', a privately chartered special train composed of two Cravens two-car diesel multiple units.

The 'Fakenham Flyer' proved to be the last passenger train to visit the town, as the station was closed completely early in the following year. The railway land was far too valuable to stay derelict for long, and by 1988 the station site had vanished under housing development. One level crossing gate and goods platform have since vanished, but the other gate has been preserved and stands back from the road among the retirement bungalows now covering the former railway land. The nearby Great Eastern pub is, however, boarded up and empty, as if to erase all memories of the railway. *RJA/DGS*

To the crowds of people milling around Fakenham station to see the 'Fakenham Flyer' the whole concept of a passenger train to the town was a novelty. A generation earlier, the railway was an accepted part of everyday life, as this charming scene, probably dating from the 1950s, shows. *Adrian Vaughan Collection*

WIGHTON was an undistinguished halt about half a mile from the village. The station was and is approached by a track from the Fakenham–Wells road, and is probably as basic a station as you can get; passengers alighting here had to travel in a specified coach because of the limited platform length. It is seen here on closure day, 3 October 1964.

I sat on an overgrown embankment in the late summer of 1990 to get this picture of the narrow gauge train on its way from Walsingham to Wells. The new railway runs a distance of approximately 5 miles and claims to be the longest $10^1/4$-inch narrow gauge railway in the country. *RJA/DGS*

WELLS-NEXT-THE-SEA boasted a compact little terminus with its freight facilities rubbing shoulders with the loco servicing area. The van on the extreme left peers from the goods shed, which was also the loco shed building, whilst the proximity of the cattle pens to the turntable and water tower makes one wonder how the beasts reacted to the sounds of steam engines being serviced! A 'D16/3' 4-4-0 waits by the turntable in August 1956.

Today we have yet another industrial estate, the fate which has befallen so many redundant station sites! Part of the mill building survives, but is now an antiques centre. A good clue here is the road name 'Great Eastern Way'.
W.J. Naunton/DGS

STANHOE: Waiting for the train at Stanhoe on the Wells to Heacham line shortly before closure in June 1952. The smart young man, station cat, rudimentary shelter and oil lamps are all worthy of note, as the track curves away into the distance across the open North Norfolk countryside. Unusually, Stanhoe station had no sidings and was therefore a 'passenger only' station; however, the occasional goods train continued to pass through on its way to Burnham Market until 1965.

After the line closed, Stanhoe station was converted into a private house. Although the shelter has gone, the station building and wooden hut are little changed externally. The dip two-thirds of the way along the platform has become a bit more pronounced, and the whole site has a considerably more sylvan air about it. *D. Thompson/DGS*

WENDLING: Returning to Dereham and taking the Kings Lynn line, here is the village station at Wendling, slumbering in the morning sunshine in July 1964. A westbound train is signalled, and a solitary prospective passenger paces the platform.

Turn to the north off the old A47 trunk road some 4 miles west of Dereham along an unclassified road which passes over the Dereham bypass, then look towards Swaffham and you are looking down on the site of Wendling station. To the left, at right angles to the bypass, there are some bungalows; the one visible here is in the same row as the one in the earlier picture, which looks to be of an earlier design (the old goods shed masks the site of this newer bungalow). *D. Thompson/DGS*

WYMONDHAM: South of Dereham was this country junction, where the lines to Dereham and Forncett left the Thetford–Norwich route. A typical local train of the 1950s pauses on the last lap of its journey to Norwich, with 'D16/3' 4-4-0 No 62522 at the head.

Wymondham station became unstaffed in the mid-1960s and the flint-built building fell into a state of disrepair. It has now been restored and is used as a piano showroom and period tea-room. In essence the scene has changed little over the years, as a Class '56' No 56065 heads towards Norwich with a Redland stone train. *W.J. Naunton/DGS*

THETFORD: The plain unrelieved blue livery of the 1970s is now thankfully only a memory, although no doubt some will recall it with affection! During that period, a down train leaves Thetford for Norwich, formed of a mixture of Metro-Cammell, Cravens and Gloucester RC&W diesel multiple unit vehicles.

The line through Thetford had been opened during the 1840s as part of the first through route from London to Norwich, but by the mid-1970s was used largely by stopping local services, with the occasional through trains to the Midlands or North. The line south to Bury, the southern section of the Thetford & Watton Railway, lost its passenger service in 1953, but retained a goods service until 1960. From the late 1980s onwards, however, the cross-country services were much improved with the use of 'Sprinters', and the summer 1991 timetable provided a virtually hourly service throughout the day between Norwich and either the North West or Birmingham. One such train, formed of a Class '158' 'Express' unit, leaves Thetford for Norwich, as a Metro-Cammell DMU enters with a Cambridge train. *D.C. Pearce/DGS*

WRETHAM & HOCKHAM: Opened as part of the Thetford & Watton Railway in 1869, the branch northwards from Thetford to Swaffham was taken over by the Great Eastern Railway 11 years later, and became another typical GER branch line. It is interesting to compare the varying fortunes of the four intermediate stations on the line, starting at the southernmost, Wretham & Hockham, where the station platform is showing signs of neglect as a 'last day' train pulls away on 13 June 1964.

Visited in October 1990, the station is in private occupation. The owner has put in a lot of work here and the station buildings are in excellent shape, having formerly been owned by the last station master. I was told that the platform was beyond repair and had to be demolished, although the lip remains. The original small lamp hut survives and is seen along the platform at the rear, while the trackbed across the road is now a private garden with a lawn and conifer trees, providing nothing to indicate that a railway ever ran here. *RJA/DGS*

WATTON: After passing through Stow Bedon (see page 6), we arrive at Watton, the principal town served by the line, but even here the arrival of the afternoon train on the final day produces only a solitary onlooker. The platforms here were staggered, and the train is passing the down platform before coming to a stand at the up.

Following closure the station site was totally redeveloped, and an Ordnance Survey map proved useful to find it, a quarter of a mile out of the town on the Norwich Road. The platform area is part of a Council depot, whilst the yard has disappeared under an industrial estate. A plaque on the wall of the building on the right reminds passers-by that this is the site of the railway station, while the imposing former station hotel looks out on a much changed scene. *Both RJA*

HOLME HALE: 'One and a half to Swaffham, please.' The porter shepherds his two customers and their pram towards the morning train from Thetford as it pulls into Holme Hale station on 17 September 1962. Both the friendliness of the rural branch line and the reason for its latter-day unprofitablility are shown in this scene.

Holme Hale is still a well-kept station with signal cabin intact. On the north side, the old goods shed has been converted into an attractive dwelling house, while alongside is a well preserved goods van painted in bauxite and sporting the initials LMS (not its original lettering). A weathervane with a locomotive design completes the scene
RJA/DGS

SWAFFHAM: Until 1964, Swaffham, on the Dereham to Kings Lynn route, was the junction for the branch line to Thetford. The destination blind shows that the DMU, waiting, perhaps optimistically, for custom on 30 March 1959, is bound for the branch. Passenger services on the Dereham to Kings Lynn section outlasted those on the branch by only four years, and Swaffham station closed completely in September 1968.

Twenty-two years later the station building appears substantially intact, and there is evidence of renovation and extension to the original structure. The yard, like so many others in small East Anglian towns, has become enveloped in an industrial estate. *A.E. Bennett/DGS*

The M&GN

GORLESTON-ON-SEA: A joint venture between the M&GN and the GER, the Norfolk & Suffolk Joint Railway from Yarmouth to Lowestoft did not open until 1903. Traffic never matched the ambitions of the builders, and the comprehensive station facilities were rarely taxed. A Derby lightweight DMU set heading a Metro-Cammell unit appears lost within Gorleston-on-Sea station in the late 'fifties.

After a life of only 67 years the line was closed entirely, and in 1991 the site of Gorleston station was being incorporated in a new road scheme. Southwards towards Lowestoft the area has been landscaped, and one can only hope for a future improvement on the northward view! Only the distant road bridge survives as a reminder of the railway. *M&GN Circle, E. Tuddenham/RJA*

HOPTON-ON-SEA. The Norfolk & Suffolk Joint Committee believed in lavish station facilities, but in most cases the traffic never really materialised. Only a handful of passengers will patronise this Derby lightweight DMU which is arriving at Hopton-on-Sea on a Yarmouth to Lowestoft working in September 1962. At this time the line was enjoying a brief final flourish, handling all the East Suffolk line Yarmouth traffic following the closure of the direct line from Beccles three years earlier.

This is not an easy site to find nowadays, a housing estate having been built across the track. The station master's house still stands, with a visible clue near the door, and a friendly (railway enthusiast) policeman pointed out the old gates to the goods yard to the right of the station master's house; but it is none the less almost impossible to envisage yesteryear's scene. *M&GN Circle, E. Tuddenham/DGS*

YARMOUTH BEACH: The 1923 Grouping scarcely affected the M&GN, which remained an independent concern until 1936. Following the LNER takeover, many of the former M&GN locos lingered on for a few years before being replaced; here, renumbered in the duplicate list and bearing the initials of its new owners, 0-6-0T No 016 shunts at Yarmouth Beach on 14 March 1939. Beyond is another sign of the LNER influence, ex-GNR 'C12' 4-4-2T No 4015 which had been imported to handle trains to Lowestoft. No 016 was to survive another ten years, coming into British Railways ownership before being withdrawn in August 1949. The 'Joint' outlasted the loco by less than a decade, and by August 1959 Yarmouth Beach station was trackless and desolate.

Since then the station area has been a coach and car park, utilising the original station buildings and offices until the late 1980s. Unfortunately my 1991 photograph coincided with a heavy summer shower, and looking across where the goods yards once stood, only the houses in the background are identifiable. Passing holidaymakers probably thought that I was mad taking a photograph of a car park in the pouring rain! *H.C. Casserley/DGS*

STALHAM: In addition to trains to Melton Constable and points further west, certain 'short' workings operated from Yarmouth Beach, terminating at intermediate stations such as Potter Heigham and Aylsham. One such train was the Wednesdays and Saturdays only 12 noon from Yarmouth to Stalham, which is seen here awaiting its 1.05 pm return to Yarmouth at the well-kept station on 27 August 1958. The four Gresley coaches are headed by Ivatt 'Mogul' No 43157.

Tucked away in a corner at the junction of the busy A149 and the B1151 to Sea Palling, Stalham station has in its retirement become a Council depot with the usual debris which accumulates in such places. Much of the goods yard and trackbed is a car park with an extension for overflow during the summer season, although it was nowhere near full when we visited it. The road bridge has been swept away in new road development. *M&GN Circle, E. Tuddenham/DGS*

MUNDESLEY-ON-SEA station was a latecomer to the railway map, the branch from North Walsham having only been opened as late as 1898. On 15 May 1960 'J15' 0-6-0 No 65469 stands in the station, the loco and branch having been hired by enthusiasts of the Norfolk Railway Society for a day's driving and firing instruction; the amateur enginemen certainly appear to be producing a good head of steam! One of several camping coaches based at Mundesley in the latter years stands in the bay platform, while a couple of coal wagons occupy the goods yard.

Traffic on the line never justified the station's three through platforms and a bay, and the service from North Walsham was withdrawn in October 1964, a victim of the Beeching Report; goods traffic finished later in the year. In the 1991 picture a lady cleans her car on a housing estate on the outskirts of Mundesley, probably unaware that the railway once occupied the land. Only the roof of the distant white-painted building in the 1960 picture provides a common element in the two views. *W.J. Naunton/RJA*

110

OVERSTRAND: The Norfolk & Suffolk Joint line from Mundesley to Cromer had a life of only some 55 years, closing completely in April 1953. On the last day of services, ex-GER 'F6' 2-4-2T No 67228 and two GER coaches forming the 12.05 from Cromer leave Overstrand station.

Not too easy to find today, a couple of miles out of Cromer on the B1159 opposite a small garage a stony private road leads up to the station. This is now private land but a footpath passes near the east side of the old station. The subway under the trackbed is still intact, but even more extraordinary is the covered walkway from the platform to the subway which is also still in existence and used, I believe, as some form of glasshouse. *M&GN Circle, E. Tuddenham/DGS*

RUNTON WEST JUNCTION: The signalman at Runton West Junction near Cromer prepares to hand over the tablet for the single-line section on to Sheringham. Cromer Beach, the former M&GN station in the resort, is a terminus, and trains from Norwich to Sheringham have to reverse there, although at one time an avoiding line ran from Runton West Junction to Newstead Lane Junction, forming a triangle. The Brush Type 2 in the picture has no doubt run round its train at Cromer Beach before continuing its journey. To the right the tracks of the avoiding line to Newstead Lane Junction appear dull and unused, thus dating the picture at around 1960/1, the spur having closed in the former year.

On 1 June 1991, a Class '158' unit passes the site of Runton West Junction box. The brand new 'Sprinter' is filling in time on local workings before going into service on the cross-country routes from Norwich to the Midlands and the North. To train crews and passengers alike, the contrast with the 30-year-old Metro-Cammell trains normally used on the Sheringham line was no doubt noticeable! The route of the avoiding line has vanished beneath the trees, but the depression in the cutting side to the left of the picture indicates where the signal box once stood. *M&GN Circle, E. Tuddenham/RJA*

SHERINGHAM: The station at Sheringham was shared by the GER and the M&GN from 1906 onwards. A DMU, possibly working on the Norwich Thorpe–Sheringham–Melton Constable–Norwich City circuit, stands at the platform on 28 February 1959.

From 1964 onwards Sheringham became the terminus of a single-line branch from Cromer, and as the station facilities were far too large for this remaining service a basic single-line platform was built a little nearer Cromer. The redundant facilities were taken over by preservationists, and the station is now the headquarters of the North Norfolk Railway. On the left-hand platform, the original buildings and canopy survive, while from the right-hand platform a small boy admires the railway's former 'Brighton Belle' Pullman car. *A.E. Bennett/RJA*

WEYBOURNE: The closure of the M&GN as a through route deprived the still substantial freight traffic from Norwich City of a direct route to the Midlands and beyond. Goods trains from Norwich had therefore to travel some 60 miles via Melton Constable and Cromer before getting back to Norwich Thorpe and its links with the rest of the country (see Themelthorpe, page 90). With the North Sea in the background, 'WD' 2-8-0 No 90559, a remarkably clean member of the class, heads one such train down the bank towards Weybourne on a summer's day in 1959.

In the summer of 1991 the first and last trains of the day on the North Norfolk Railway are diesel operated, and here we renew acquaintance with one of the little German four-wheeled railbuses which operated out of Cambridge in the 1960s, on this occasion E79963. The section of line from Weybourne to Holt was lifted after closure in 1964, and was subsequently relaid by the North Norfolk Railway. The concrete platelayers' hut has survived all the changes, whilst beyond the railway the traditional field pattern is substantially unchanged. *M&GN Circle, E. Tuddenham/RJA*

HOLT: The M&GN's Cromer line survived the otherwise wholesale 1959 closure and passenger trains continued to run to Melton Constable from Sheringham until April 1964. On the final afternoon of services, two Metro-Cammell DMUs pass at Holt station, the last daylight use of the loop there. *RJA*

Freight lingered on to the end of 1964, and the track was then lifted. During the '70s the derelict station languished before the bypass was built. The preserved North Norfolk Railway had hopes of extending their line to the old station but the realignment of the road and removal of a dangerous rail bridge put paid to these hopes. However, a good compromise has been reached with a new station on the north side of the road, a short distance from the town. *D.C. Pearce*

The old station in October 1988, and all has been swept away, although a good clue is still in sight — the mill on the right remains, looking down on a very different scene. *DGS*

CORPUSTY: On the line between North Walsham and Melton Constable, Corpusty was a typical country station. Seen here from the roadbridge, a short goods yard and some cattle pens are visible. At least Corpusty station was in the village, which could not be said of too many stations on the M&GN — a traveller once enquired at a local pub why a certain station was so far from the village, and was told 'because it's near the railway'. From Corpusty the line was doubled for some 18 miles to Raynham Park.

The same view in October 1988, and the whole area is under grass. It is now a sports centre with sleeping accommodation provided at the station house. A lone stroller exercises his dog. *Ray Meek Collection/DGS*

DRAYTON: After the closure of the majority of the M&GN system, the Norwich branch continued to carry quite considerable freight traffic. Even after Norwich City station itself closed, the line continued in use for the conveyance of concrete products from Lenwade and sand from Drayton. Brush Type 2 No D5579 shunts the sand train in Drayton yard on 14 April 1969, with the traditional goods sheds and loading dock well in evidence. This traffic survived a year or two longer, but by 1973 the tracklifting gang was at work here.

Nineteen years later, in August 1988, the area is occupied by a small industrial estate, although the houses in the background are easily identifiable. With a little hindsight, how useful a light railway would be now with the vast Thorpe Marriott estate just half a mile away, which makes a busy road even busier. *RJA/DGS*

MELTON CONSTABLE (1): The activity at Melton West Junction belies the fact that this picture was taken on the very last day of the M&GN as a through route. A '4MT' 2-6-0 pulls away from the station stop with the final through train from Yarmouth Beach to Leicester and Birmingham, as a down freight arrives with another '4MT' at the head. The Cromer line curves away to the right, above the ex-GER restaurant car which provided refreshments on the 'Leicester'.

An incredible difference in today's viewpoint! The fields are under cultivation and the line of electric poles almost bisects the angle of the old lines to Holt and Cromer. However, the tower known as Belle Vue is just visible in the left background of both pictures — originally a smock mill, it is alleged to have a fine view of Norwich and the sea. *A.E. Bennett/DGS*

MELTON CONSTABLE (2): Another of the versatile Ivatt 'Moguls', South Lynn's No 43107, stands at Melton Constable with a Peterborough to Yarmouth train alongside a splendid signal post controlling the goods line.

Yesteryear's 'Crewe of North Norfolk' is today an industrial estate. Using the house on the right as a marker, I stood (with permission) in the spring of 1991 among a line of small conifers just about where the platform ended; where the '4MT' once stood a car was parked beside a brick-built club house. *Doug Watts/DGS*

THURSFORD: Ivatt 'Mogul' No 43154 passes a typical M&GN signal box and crossing gates as it runs into the country station at Thursford in 1958. *M&GN Circle, E. Tuddenham*

The second picture of the sequence shows the derelict station in the mid-'sixties. *DGS*

'Where exactly did the signal box stand?' I asked the elderly gentleman exercising his dog. 'Right here,' and he indicated a spot some 20 yards in front of where I was standing. The old goods shed is now used as a Council depot, and the house in the 1958 picture is just visible beyond the trees. *DGS*

FAKENHAM WEST: Despite early dieselisation elsewhere in the area, the M&GN, except for the Norwich and Cromer branches, remained very much a steam railway to the end. During the final years, however, two of the Norwich branch services were extended through to Fakenham West, thus providing a rare diesel railcar turn on the main line. This Metro-Cammell unit has just crossed from the up to the down platform at Fakenham, and is about to return to Melton Constable.

The trackbed now leads to the Gallows Sports Centre and Caravan Park, and a builders merchant's yards cover the whole area. However, a small length of platform remains, under the lip of which a plate reminds us that the Lynn & Fakenham Railway reached here in 1876; this momento was very much the initiative of the late Peter Fitzjohn. The concrete base of the footbridge steps remain on the old platform. *Doug Watts/DGS*

In the spring of 1965, whilst I was taking photographs at Fakenham West station, a trio of workmen arrived and promptly set about the signal box, which was positioned just across the road. I was advised to hurry up or there wouldn't be much left — a case of being in the right place at the right time! *DGS*

121

RAYNHAM PARK: A feature of the M&GN was the Whitaker tablet exchange apparatus which enabled single-line tablets to be exchanged at speed, thus obviating a potential source of delay on the long single-line sections. The apparatus is ready for use beside the cab as '4F' 0-6-0 No 43954 passes through Raynham Park before running on to the single-line section to East Rudham. The '4Fs' were regular visitors to the M&GN, particularly on summer Saturdays, and this Nottingham-based loco is heading homewards with the 8.19 am train from Yarmouth Beach to Chesterfield on 2 August 1958.

On 13 July 1991 the summer meeting of the M&GN Circle was held at Raynham Park station and the opportunity was taken to match the old photograph taken from the signal box steps. The station master's house on the other side of the trackbed is clearly visible, the station building and signal box are in private occupation and in excellent repair, and a good effort has been made to preserve the old railway atmosphere in a sylvan setting. *M&GN Circle, E. Tuddenham/DGS*

EAST RUDHAM: Seen again from the signal box, Class '4MT' No 43110 stands at East Rudham station with a lengthy up cattle special on 21 May 1958. These Ivatt-designed locos replaced a miscellaneous selection of ageing motive power on the M&GN section from the early 1950s, and proved very successful on all types of traffic. Those allocated to the M&GN were fitted with the tablet exchange apparatus for use on single-line sections, and this can be seen fixed to the side of the tender of 43110.

Following the closure of the majority of the M&GN to passenger traffic on 28 February 1959, East Rudham became the terminus of a freight line from Kings Lynn, and for a few years generated a worthwhile grain traffic. Final closure came in 1968, and today the yard and trackbed are in commercial use. The goods shed in the background is still standing, while the station buildings, although empty, were in a good state of repair and had changed but little over the years. When photographed in April 1991, an estate agent's sign indicated that a buyer would be welcomed. *M&GN Circle, E. Tuddenham/RJA*

GAYTON ROAD: On a bright winter morning in the late 1950s, Ivatt '4MT' No 43158 sweeps through Gayton Road station in fine style with the Yarmouth Beach to Birmingham expresses, an old GER buffet car rattling along at the front of the train. The tall Great Northern somersault signal with its repeater arm was a distinctive feature of the station, and the goods yard was still serving its scattered rural community.

With the passage of time a young wood has enveloped the site of the station, and only the platform end emerges from the greenery. The whole area is being landscaped, and the elevated 1959 viewpoint has been bulldozed away; on the right, however, the white shed with the sliding door has resisted change. *M&GN Circle, E. Tuddenham/RJA*

SOUTH LYNN: With its loco shed and marshalling yards, South Lynn was an important traffic centre on the M&GN. There was also a physical connection with the GER lines into that company's Kings Lynn station, over which a regular push-pull service operated. In the late 1950s, Class 'C12' 4-4-2T No 67386 passes some early examples of colour light signals as it leaves South Lynn with this shuttle service at the start of its 5-minute journey to the former GE station.

The station at South Lynn was demolished soon after the 1959 closure, but goods trains still run through the former complex to serve an adjacent sugar beet factory. In October 1984 Class '47' No 47097 was photographed on the surviving tracks, shunting wagons of limestone from Wirksworth and oil tankers from Shellhaven, both bound for the beet factory. To connect the pictures, the '47' is standing on the line seen disappearing to the left of the 'C12', and one of the gateposts in the foreground of the 1984 photo can just be made out above the top right-hand corner of the black hut to the left of the earlier view. An exact duplication of the previous photograph would reveal little but an expanse of neglected waste ground and the distant Kings Lynn bypass. This somewhat bleak scene is little altered today. *Dr I.C. Allen/RJA*

SUTTON BRIDGE: A Great Northern-style somersault signal allows Ivatt '4MT' 2-6-0 No 43142 to take its westbound train of ex-LMS coaches over the swing bridge at Sutton Bridge and into the station. The railway used one side of the bridge over the Nene, while road traffic was concentrated on the other side. Even when this picture was taken in the 1950s, the resultant bottleneck caused considerable delays to road traffic.

Following the closure of the 'Joint', the former railway side became the westbound carriageway of the A17 trunk road, but hold-ups are still common here, especially during the summer. This June 1991 picture was taken during a rare break in the traffic. Interestingly, the level crossing gatepost and distinctive M&GN criss-cross fencing still survive by the bush to the right of the bridge. *Dr I.C. Allen/DGS*

MURROW: It was rare in the UK for two railway lines to cross on the level, so the situation at Murrow, where two joint lines crossed on the level, must have been unique. Ivatt '4MT' 2-6-0 No 43081 heads a lightweight M&GN line freight across the GN/GE Joint March–Spalding line on 13 October 1960, past the modern brick-built signal box. This had replaced an earlier structure which was destroyed in the early hours of 4 October 1941, when a coal train on the M&GN rammed a GN/GE freight which had overrun signals and stopped on the crossing.

The M&GN route continued to handle goods traffic until 1965 whilst the GN/GE line survived until November 1982, although its station at Murrow, latterly known as Murrow West, had closed as early as 1953. The tracks on both routes have now been lifted, but the derelict signal box still stands, surveying the overgrown trackbed. A curious feature is the junction signal still guarding a non-existent junction — in the last two years it has sprouted arms. *M&GN Circle, K.A. Ladbury/DGS*

INDEX OF LOCATIONS